Animal Welfare Act 2006

CHAPTER 45

Explanatory Notes are available separately

AF719450

GRAN*GIS* UK Publishing

Adapted and published by GRANGIS (Grand Register Library).
Online: www.grangis.com
E-mail: contact@grangis.com

In this version:
ISBN: 979-8-88559-003-7

Note: This is the original version (as it was originally enacted). Title, sub-title and the generated date is as marked on the pages.

Animal Welfare Act 2006

CHAPTER 45

ANIMAL WELFARE ACT 2006

Introductory

Prevention of harm

Promotion of welfare

Licensing and registration

Codes of practice

Animal Welfare Act 2006

2006 CHAPTER 45

An Act to make provision about animal welfare; and for connected purposes. [8th November 2006]

BE IT ENACTED by the Queen's most Excellent Majesty, by and with the advice and consent of the Lords Spiritual and Temporal, and Commons, in this present Parliament assembled, and by the authority of the same, as follows:—

Introductory

1 Animals to which the Act applies

(1) In this Act, except subsections (4) and (5), "animal" means a vertebrate other than man.

(2) Nothing in this Act applies to an animal while it is in its foetal or embryonic form.

(3) The appropriate national authority may by regulations for all or any of the purposes of this Act—

- (a) extend the definition of "animal" so as to include invertebrates of any description;
- (b) make provision in lieu of subsection (2) as respects any invertebrates included in the definition of "animal";
- (c) amend subsection (2) to extend the application of this Act to an animal from such earlier stage of its development as may be specified in the regulations.

(4) The power under subsection (3)(a) or (c) may only be exercised if the appropriate national authority is satisfied, on the basis of scientific evidence, that animals of the kind concerned are capable of experiencing pain or suffering.

(5) In this section, "vertebrate" means any animal of the Sub-phylum Vertebrata of the Phylum Chordata and "invertebrate" means any animal not of that Sub-phylum.

2 "Protected animal"

An animal is a "protected animal" for the purposes of this Act if—

(a) it is of a kind which is commonly domesticated in the British Islands,

(b) it is under the control of man whether on a permanent or temporary basis, or

(c) it is not living in a wild state.

3 Responsibility for animals

(1) In this Act, references to a person responsible for an animal are to a person responsible for an animal whether on a permanent or temporary basis.

(2) In this Act, references to being responsible for an animal include being in charge of it.

(3) For the purposes of this Act, a person who owns an animal shall always be regarded as being a person who is responsible for it.

(4) For the purposes of this Act, a person shall be treated as responsible for any animal for which a person under the age of 16 years of whom he has actual care and control is responsible.

Prevention of harm

4 Unnecessary suffering

(1) A person commits an offence if—

(a) an act of his, or a failure of his to act, causes an animal to suffer,

(b) he knew, or ought reasonably to have known, that the act, or failure to act, would have that effect or be likely to do so,

(c) the animal is a protected animal, and

(d) the suffering is unnecessary.

(2) A person commits an offence if—

(a) he is responsible for an animal,

(b) an act, or failure to act, of another person causes the animal to suffer,

(c) he permitted that to happen or failed to take such steps (whether by way of supervising the other person or otherwise) as were reasonable in all the circumstances to prevent that happening, and

(d) the suffering is unnecessary.

(3) The considerations to which it is relevant to have regard when determining for the purposes of this section whether suffering is unnecessary include—

(a) whether the suffering could reasonably have been avoided or reduced;

(b) whether the conduct which caused the suffering was in compliance with any relevant enactment or any relevant provisions of a licence or code of practice issued under an enactment;

(c) whether the conduct which caused the suffering was for a legitimate purpose, such as—

(i) the purpose of benefiting the animal, or

(ii) the purpose of protecting a person, property or another animal;

(d) whether the suffering was proportionate to the purpose of the conduct concerned;

(e) whether the conduct concerned was in all the circumstances that of a reasonably competent and humane person.

(4) Nothing in this section applies to the destruction of an animal in an appropriate and humane manner.

5 Mutilation

(1) A person commits an offence if—

(a) he carries out a prohibited procedure on a protected animal;

(b) he causes such a procedure to be carried out on such an animal.

(2) A person commits an offence if—

(a) he is responsible for an animal,

(b) another person carries out a prohibited procedure on the animal, and

(c) he permitted that to happen or failed to take such steps (whether by way of supervising the other person or otherwise) as were reasonable in all the circumstances to prevent that happening.

(3) References in this section to the carrying out of a prohibited procedure on an animal are to the carrying out of a procedure which involves interference with the sensitive tissues or bone structure of the animal, otherwise than for the purpose of its medical treatment.

(4) Subsections (1) and (2) do not apply in such circumstances as the appropriate national authority may specify by regulations.

(5) Before making regulations under subsection (4), the appropriate national authority shall consult such persons appearing to the authority to represent any interests concerned as the authority considers appropriate.

(6) Nothing in this section applies to the removal of the whole or any part of a dog's tail.

6 Docking of dogs' tails

(1) A person commits an offence if—

(a) he removes the whole or any part of a dog's tail, otherwise than for the purpose of its medical treatment;

(b) he causes the whole or any part of a dog's tail to be removed by another person, otherwise than for the purpose of its medical treatment.

(2) A person commits an offence if—

(a) he is responsible for a dog,

(b) another person removes the whole or any part of the dog's tail, otherwise than for the purpose of its medical treatment, and

(c) he permitted that to happen or failed to take such steps (whether by way of supervising the other person or otherwise) as were reasonable in all the circumstances to prevent that happening.

(3) Subsections (1) and (2) do not apply if the dog is a certified working dog that is not more than 5 days old.

(4) For the purposes of subsection (3), a dog is a certified working dog if a veterinary surgeon has certified, in accordance with regulations made by the appropriate national authority, that the first and second conditions mentioned below are met.

(5) The first condition referred to in subsection (4) is that there has been produced to the veterinary surgeon such evidence as the appropriate national authority may by regulations require for the purpose of showing that the dog is likely to be used for work in connection with—

(a) law enforcement,

(b) activities of Her Majesty's armed forces,

(c) emergency rescue,

(d) lawful pest control, or

(e) the lawful shooting of animals.

(6) The second condition referred to in subsection (4) is that the dog is of a type specified for the purposes of this subsection by regulations made by the appropriate national authority.

(7) It is a defence for a person accused of an offence under subsection (1) or (2) to show that he reasonably believed that the dog was one in relation to which subsection (3) applies.

(8) A person commits an offence if—

(a) he owns a subsection (3) dog, and

(b) fails to take reasonable steps to secure that, before the dog is 3 months old, it is identified as a subsection (3) dog in accordance with regulations made by the appropriate national authority.

(9) A person commits an offence if—

(a) he shows a dog at an event to which members of the public are admitted on payment of a fee,

(b) the dog's tail has been wholly or partly removed (in England and Wales or elsewhere), and

(c) removal took place on or after the commencement day.

(10) Where a dog is shown only for the purpose of demonstrating its working ability, subsection (9) does not apply if the dog is a subsection (3) dog.

(11) It is a defence for a person accused of an offence under subsection (9) to show that he reasonably believed—

(a) that the event was not one to which members of the public were admitted on payment of an entrance fee,

(b) that the removal took place before the commencement day, or

(c) that the dog was one in relation to which subsection (10) applies.

(12) A person commits an offence if he knowingly gives false information to a veterinary surgeon in connection with the giving of a certificate for the purposes of this section.

(13) The appropriate national authority may by regulations make provision about the functions of inspectors in relation to—

(a) certificates for the purposes of this section, and

(b) the identification of dogs as subsection (3) dogs.

(14) Power to make regulations under this section includes power—

(a) to make different provision for different cases, and

(b) to make incidental, supplementary, consequential or transitional provision or savings.

(15) Before making regulations under this section, the appropriate national authority shall consult such persons appearing to the authority to represent any interests concerned as the authority considers appropriate.

(16) In this section—

"commencement day" means the day on which this section comes into force;

"subsection (3) dog" means a dog whose tail has, on or after the commencement day, been wholly or partly removed without contravening subsection (1), because of the application of subsection (3).

7 Administration of poisons etc.

(1) A person commits an offence if, without lawful authority or reasonable excuse, he—

(a) administers any poisonous or injurious drug or substance to a protected animal, knowing it to be poisonous or injurious, or

(b) causes any poisonous or injurious drug or substance to be taken by a protected animal, knowing it to be poisonous or injurious.

(2) A person commits an offence if—

(a) he is responsible for an animal,

(b) without lawful authority or reasonable excuse, another person administers a poisonous or injurious drug or substance to the animal or causes the animal to take such a drug or substance, and

(c) he permitted that to happen or, knowing the drug or substance to be poisonous or injurious, he failed to take such steps (whether by way of supervising the other person or otherwise) as were reasonable in all the circumstances to prevent that happening.

(3) In this section, references to a poisonous or injurious drug or substance include a drug or substance which, by virtue of the quantity or manner in which it is administered or taken, has the effect of a poisonous or injurious drug or substance.

8 Fighting etc.

(1) A person commits an offence if he—

(a) causes an animal fight to take place, or attempts to do so;

(b) knowingly receives money for admission to an animal fight;

(c) knowingly publicises a proposed animal fight;

(d) provides information about an animal fight to another with the intention of enabling or encouraging attendance at the fight;

(e) makes or accepts a bet on the outcome of an animal fight or on the likelihood of anything occurring or not occurring in the course of an animal fight;

(f) takes part in an animal fight;

(g) has in his possession anything designed or adapted for use in connection with an animal fight with the intention of its being so used;
(h) keeps or trains an animal for use for in connection with an animal fight;
(i) keeps any premises for use for an animal fight.

(2) A person commits an offence if, without lawful authority or reasonable excuse, he is present at an animal fight.

(3) A person commits an offence if, without lawful authority or reasonable excuse, he—
(a) knowingly supplies a video recording of an animal fight,
(b) knowingly publishes a video recording of an animal fight,
(c) knowingly shows a video recording of an animal fight to another, or
(d) possesses a video recording of an animal fight, knowing it to be such a recording, with the intention of supplying it.

(4) Subsection (3) does not apply if the video recording is of an animal fight that took place—
(a) outside Great Britain, or
(b) before the commencement date.

(5) Subsection (3) does not apply—
(a) in the case of paragraph (a), to the supply of a video recording for inclusion in a programme service;
(b) in the case of paragraph (b) or (c), to the publication or showing of a video recording by means of its inclusion in a programme service;
(c) in the case of paragraph (d), by virtue of intention to supply for inclusion in a programme service.

(6) Provision extending the application of an offence under subsection (3), so far as relating to the provision of information society services, may be made under section 2(2) of the European Communities Act 1972 (c. 68) (powers to implement Community obligations by regulations) notwithstanding the limits imposed by paragraph 1(1)(d) of Schedule 2 to that Act on the penalties with which an offence may be punishable on summary conviction.

(7) In this section—

"animal fight" means an occasion on which a protected animal is placed with an animal, or with a human, for the purpose of fighting, wrestling or baiting;

'"commencement date" means the date on which subsection (3) comes into force;

"information society services" has the meaning given in Article 2(a) of Directive 2000/31/EC of the European Parliament and of the Council of 8 June 2000 on certain legal aspects of information society services, in particular electronic commerce in the Internal Market (Directive on electronic commerce);

"programme service" has the same meaning as in the Communications Act 2003 (c. 21);

"video recording" means a recording, in any form, from which a moving image may by any means be reproduced and includes data stored on a computer disc or by other electronic means which is capable of conversion into a moving image.

(8) In this section—

(a) references to supplying or publishing a video recording are to supplying or publishing a video recording in any manner, including, in relation to a video recording in the form of data stored electronically, by means of transmitting such data;

(b) references to showing a video recording are to showing a moving image reproduced from a video recording by any means.

Promotion of welfare

9 Duty of person responsible for animal to ensure welfare

(1) A person commits an offence if he does not take such steps as are reasonable in all the circumstances to ensure that the needs of an animal for which he is responsible are met to the extent required by good practice.

(2) For the purposes of this Act, an animal's needs shall be taken to include—

(a) its need for a suitable environment,

(b) its need for a suitable diet,

(c) its need to be able to exhibit normal behaviour patterns,

(d) any need it has to be housed with, or apart from, other animals, and

(e) its need to be protected from pain, suffering, injury and disease.

(3) The circumstances to which it is relevant to have regard when applying subsection (1) include, in particular—

(a) any lawful purpose for which the animal is kept, and

(b) any lawful activity undertaken in relation to the animal.

(4) Nothing in this section applies to the destruction of an animal in an appropriate and humane manner.

10 Improvement notices

(1) If an inspector is of the opinion that a person is failing to comply with section 9(1), he may serve on the person a notice which—

(a) states that he is of that opinion,

(b) specifies the respects in which he considers the person is failing to comply with that provision,

(c) specifies the steps he considers need to be taken in order to comply with the provision,

(d) specifies a period for the taking of those steps, and

(e) explains the effect of subsections (2) and (3).

(2) Where a notice under subsection (1) ("an improvement notice") is served, no proceedings for an offence under section 9(1) may be instituted before the end of the period specified for the purposes of subsection (1)(d) ("the compliance period") in respect of—

(a) the non-compliance which gave rise to the notice, or

(b) any continuation of that non-compliance.

(3) If the steps specified in an improvement notice are taken at any time before the end of the compliance period, no proceedings for an offence under section 9(1) may be instituted in respect of—

(a) the non-compliance which gave rise to the notice, or

(b) any continuation of that non-compliance prior to the taking of the steps specified in the notice.

(4) An inspector may extend, or further extend, the compliance period specified in an improvement notice.

11 Transfer of animals by way of sale or prize to persons under 16

(1) A person commits an offence if he sells an animal to a person whom he has reasonable cause to believe to be under the age of 16 years.

(2) For the purposes of subsection (1), selling an animal includes transferring, or agreeing to transfer, ownership of the animal in consideration of entry by the transferee into another transaction.

(3) Subject to subsections (4) to (6), a person commits an offence if—

(a) he enters into an arrangement with a person whom he has reasonable cause to believe to be under the age of 16 years, and

(b) the arrangement is one under which that person has the chance to win an animal as a prize.

(4) A person does not commit an offence under subsection (3) if—

(a) he enters into the arrangement in the presence of the person with whom the arrangement is made, and

(b) he has reasonable cause to believe that the person with whom the arrangement is made is accompanied by a person who is not under the age of 16 years.

(5) A person does not commit an offence under subsection (3) if—

(a) he enters into the arrangement otherwise than in the presence of the person with whom the arrangement is made, and

(b) he has reasonable cause to believe that a person who has actual care and control of the person with whom the arrangement is made has consented to the arrangement.

(6) A person does not commit an offence under subsection (3) if he enters into the arrangement in a family context.

12 Regulations to promote welfare

(1) The appropriate national authority may by regulations make such provision as the authority thinks fit for the purpose of promoting the welfare of animals for which a person is responsible, or the progeny of such animals.

(2) Without prejudice to the generality of the power under subsection (1), regulations under that subsection may, in particular—

(a) make provision imposing specific requirements for the purpose of securing that the needs of animals are met;

(b) make provision to facilitate or improve co-ordination in relation to the carrying out by different persons of functions relating to the welfare of animals;

(c) make provision for the establishment of one or more bodies with functions relating to advice about the welfare of animals.

(3) Power to make regulations under subsection (1) includes power—

(a) to provide that breach of a provision of the regulations is an offence;

(b) to apply a relevant post-conviction power in relation to conviction for an offence under the regulations;

(c) to make provision for fees or other charges in relation to the carrying out of functions under the regulations;

(d) to make different provision for different cases or areas;

(e) to provide for exemptions from a provision of the regulations, either subject to specified conditions or without conditions;

(f) to make incidental, supplementary, consequential or transitional provision or savings.

(4) Power to make regulations under subsection (1) does not include power to create an offence triable on indictment or punishable with—

(a) imprisonment for a term exceeding 51 weeks, or

(b) a fine exceeding level 5 on the standard scale.

(5) Regulations under subsection (1) may provide that a specified offence under the regulations is to be treated as a relevant offence for the purposes of section 23.

(6) Before making regulations under subsection (1), the appropriate national authority shall consult such persons appearing to the authority to represent any interests concerned as the authority considers appropriate.

(7) In this section, "specified" means specified in regulations under subsection (1).

Licensing and registration

13 Licensing or registration of activities involving animals

(1) No person shall carry on an activity to which this subsection applies except under the authority of a licence for the purposes of this section.

(2) Subsection (1) applies to an activity which—

(a) involves animals for which a person is responsible, and

(b) is specified for the purposes of the subsection by regulations made by the appropriate national authority.

(3) No person shall carry on an activity to which this subsection applies unless registered for the purposes of this section.

(4) Subsection (3) applies to an activity which—

(a) involves animals for which a person is responsible, and

(b) is specified for the purposes of the subsection by regulations made by the appropriate national authority.

(5) Regulations under subsection (2) or (4) may only be made for the purpose of promoting the welfare of animals for which a person is responsible, or the progeny of such animals.

(6) A person commits an offence if he contravenes subsection (1) or (3).

(7) The appropriate national authority may by regulations make provision about licences or registration for the purposes of this section.

(8) The appropriate national authority may by regulations repeal any of the following enactments (which impose licence or registration requirements in relation to activities involving animals)—

- (a) section 1(1) of the Performing Animals (Regulation) Act 1925 (c. 38);
- (b) section 1(1) of the Pet Animals Act 1951 (c. 35);
- (c) section 1(1) of the Animal Boarding Establishments Act 1963 (c. 43);
- (d) section 1(1) of the Riding Establishments Act 1964 (c. 70);
- (e) section 1(1) of the Breeding of Dogs Act 1973 (c. 60).

(9) Before making regulations under this section, the appropriate national authority shall consult such persons appearing to the authority to represent any interests concerned as the authority considers appropriate.

(10) Schedule 1 (which makes provision about regulations under this section) has effect.

Codes of practice

14 Codes of practice

(1) The appropriate national authority may issue, and may from time to time revise, codes of practice for the purpose of providing practical guidance in respect of any provision made by or under this Act.

(2) The authority responsible for issuing a code of practice under subsection (1) shall publish the code, and any revision of it, in such manner as it considers appropriate.

(3) A person's failure to comply with a provision of a code of practice issued under this section shall not of itself render him liable to proceedings of any kind.

(4) In any proceedings against a person for an offence under this Act or an offence under regulations under section 12 or 13—

- (a) failure to comply with a relevant provision of a code of practice issued under this section may be relied upon as tending to establish liability, and
- (b) compliance with a relevant provision of such a code of practice may be relied upon as tending to negative liability.

15 Making and approval of codes of practice: England

(1) Where the Secretary of State proposes to issue (or revise) a code of practice under section 14, he shall—

- (a) prepare a draft of the code (or revised code),
- (b) consult about the draft such persons appearing to him to represent any interests concerned as he considers appropriate, and

(c) consider any representations made by them.

(2) If following consultation under subsection (1) the Secretary of State decides to proceed with a draft (either in its original form or with such modifications as he thinks fit), he shall lay a copy of it before Parliament.

(3) If, within the 40-day period, either House of Parliament resolves not to approve a draft laid under subsection (2), the Secretary of State shall take no further steps in relation to it.

(4) If, within the 40-day period, neither House resolves not to approve a draft laid under subsection (2), the Secretary of State shall issue (or revise) the code in the form of the draft.

(5) A code (or revised code) shall come into force on such day as the Secretary of State may by order appoint.

(6) Subsection (3) does not prevent a new draft of a code (or revised code) from being laid before Parliament.

(7) An order under subsection (5) may include transitional provision or savings.

(8) In this section, "the 40-day period", in relation to a draft laid under subsection (2), means—

(a) if the draft is laid before the Houses on different days, the period of 40 days beginning with the later of the two days, and

(b) in any other case, the period of 40 days beginning with the day on which the draft is laid before each House,

no account being taken of any period during which Parliament is dissolved or prorogued or during which both Houses are adjourned for more than four days.

16 Making of codes of practice: Wales

(1) Where the National Assembly for Wales proposes to issue (or revise) a code of practice under section 14, it shall—

(a) prepare a draft of the code (or revised code),

(b) consult about the draft such persons appearing to it to represent any interests concerned as it considers appropriate, and

(c) consider any representations made by them.

(2) The Assembly may issue (or revise) a code either in the form of the draft prepared under subsection (1)(a) or with such modification as it thinks fit.

(3) A code (or revised code) shall come into force in accordance with its provisions.

(4) A code (or revised code) may include transitional provision or savings.

17 Revocation of codes of practice

(1) The appropriate national authority may by order revoke a code of practice issued by it under section 14.

(2) An order under subsection (1) may include transitional provision or savings.

(3) Before making an order under subsection (1), the appropriate national authority shall consult such persons appearing to the authority to represent any interests concerned as the authority considers appropriate.

(4) Subsection (3) does not apply in relation to an order revoking a code of practice in connection with its replacement by a new one.

Animals in distress

18 Powers in relation to animals in distress

(1) If an inspector or a constable reasonably believes that a protected animal is suffering, he may take, or arrange for the taking of, such steps as appear to him to be immediately necessary to alleviate the animal's suffering.

(2) Subsection (1) does not authorise destruction of an animal.

(3) If a veterinary surgeon certifies that the condition of a protected animal is such that it should in its own interests be destroyed, an inspector or a constable may—

- (a) destroy the animal where it is or take it to another place and destroy it there, or
- (b) arrange for the doing of any of the things mentioned in paragraph (a).

(4) An inspector or a constable may act under subsection (3) without the certificate of a veterinary surgeon if it appears to him—

- (a) that the condition of the animal is such that there is no reasonable alternative to destroying it, and
- (b) that the need for action is such that it is not reasonably practicable to wait for a veterinary surgeon.

(5) An inspector or a constable may take a protected animal into possession if a veterinary surgeon certifies—

- (a) that it is suffering, or
- (b) that it is likely to suffer if its circumstances do not change.

(6) An inspector or a constable may act under subsection (5) without the certificate of a veterinary surgeon if it appears to him—

- (a) that the animal is suffering or that it is likely to do so if its circumstances do not change, and
- (b) that the need for action is such that it is not reasonably practicable to wait for a veterinary surgeon.

(7) The power conferred by subsection (5) includes power to take into possession dependent offspring of an animal taken into possession under that subsection.

(8) Where an animal is taken into possession under subsection (5), an inspector or a constable may—

- (a) remove it, or arrange for it to be removed, to a place of safety;
- (b) care for it, or arrange for it to be cared for—
  - (i) on the premises where it was being kept when it was taken into possession, or
  - (ii) at such other place as he thinks fit;
- (c) mark it, or arrange for it to be marked, for identification purposes.

(9) A person acting under subsection (8)(b)(i), or under an arrangement under that provision, may make use of any equipment on the premises.

(10) A veterinary surgeon may examine and take samples from an animal for the purpose of determining whether to issue a certificate under subsection (3) or (5) with respect to the animal.

(11) If a person exercises a power under this section otherwise than with the knowledge of a person who is responsible for the animal concerned, he must, as soon as reasonably practicable after exercising the power, take such steps as are reasonable in the circumstances to bring the exercise of the power to the notice of such a person.

(12) A person commits an offence if he intentionally obstructs a person in the exercise of power conferred by this section.

(13) A magistrates' court may, on application by a person who incurs expenses in acting under this section, order that he be reimbursed by such person as it thinks fit.

(14) A person affected by a decision under subsection (13) may appeal against the decision to the Crown Court.

19 Power of entry for section 18 purposes

(1) An inspector or a constable may enter premises for the purpose of searching for a protected animal and of exercising any power under section 18 in relation to it if he reasonably believes—
 (a) that there is a protected animal on the premises, and
 (b) that the animal is suffering or, if the circumstances of the animal do not change, it is likely to suffer.

(2) Subsection (1) does not authorise entry to any part of premises which is used as a private dwelling.

(3) An inspector or a constable may (if necessary) use reasonable force in exercising the power conferred by subsection (1), but only if it appears to him that entry is required before a warrant under subsection (4) can be obtained and executed.

(4) Subject to subsection (5), a justice of the peace may, on the application of an inspector or constable, issue a warrant authorising an inspector or a constable to enter premises for the purpose mentioned in subsection (1), if necessary using reasonable force.

(5) The power to issue a warrant under subsection (4) is exercisable only if the justice of the peace is satisfied—
 (a) that there are reasonable grounds for believing that there is a protected animal on the premises and that the animal is suffering or is likely to suffer if its circumstances do not change, and
 (b) that section 52 is satisfied in relation to the premises.

20 Orders in relation to animals taken under section 18(5)

(1) A magistrates' court may order any of the following in relation to an animal taken into possession under section 18(5)—
 (a) that specified treatment be administered to the animal;
 (b) that possession of the animal be given up to a specified person;

(c) that the animal be sold;

(d) that the animal be disposed of otherwise than by way of sale;

(e) that the animal be destroyed.

(2) If an animal is taken into possession under section 18(5) when it is pregnant, the power conferred by subsection (1) shall also be exercisable in relation to any offspring that results from the pregnancy.

(3) The power conferred by subsection (1) shall be exercisable on application by—

(a) the owner of the animal, or

(b) any other person appearing to the court to have a sufficient interest in the animal.

(4) A court may not make an order under subsection (1) unless—

(a) it has given the owner of the animal an opportunity to be heard, or

(b) it is satisfied that it is not reasonably practicable to communicate with the owner.

(5) Where a court makes an order under subsection (1), it may—

(a) appoint a person to carry out, or arrange for the carrying out, of the order;

(b) give directions with respect to the carrying out of the order;

(c) confer additional powers (including power to enter premises where the animal is being kept) for the purpose of, or in connection with, the carrying out of the order;

(d) order a person to reimburse the expenses of carrying out the order.

(6) In determining how to exercise its powers under this section, the court shall have regard, amongst other things, to the desirability of protecting the animal's value and avoiding increasing any expenses which a person may be ordered to reimburse.

(7) A person commits an offence if he intentionally obstructs a person in the exercise of any power conferred by virtue of this section.

(8) If the owner of the animal is subject to a liability by virtue of section 18(13) or subsection (5)(d) above, any amount to which he is entitled as a result of sale of the animal may be reduced by an amount equal to that liability.

21 Orders under section 20: appeals

(1) Where a court makes an order under section 20(1), the owner of the animal to which the order relates may appeal against the order to the Crown Court.

(2) Nothing may be done under an order under section 20(1) unless—

(a) the period for giving notice of appeal against the order has expired, and

(b) if the order is the subject of an appeal, the appeal has been determined or withdrawn.

(3) Where the effect of an order is suspended under subsection (2)—

(a) no directions given in connection with the order shall have effect, but

(b) the court may give directions about how any animal to which the order applies is to be dealt with during the suspension.

(4) Directions under subsection (3)(b) may, in particular—

(a) appoint a person to carry out, or arrange for the carrying out, of the directions;
(b) require any person who has possession of the animal to deliver it up for the purposes of the directions;
(c) confer additional powers (including power to enter premises where the animal is being kept) for the purpose of, or in connection with, the carrying out of the directions;
(d) provide for the recovery of any expenses which are reasonably incurred in carrying out the directions.

(5) Where a court decides on an application under section 20(3)(a) not to exercise the power conferred by subsection (1) of that section, the applicant may appeal against the decision to the Crown Court.

(6) Where a court makes an order under section 20(5)(d), the person against whom the order is made may appeal against the order to the Crown Court.

Enforcement powers

22 Seizure of animals involved in fighting offences

(1) A constable may seize an animal if it appears to him that it is one in relation to which an offence under section 8(1) or (2) has been committed.

(2) A constable may enter and search premises for the purpose of exercising the power under subsection (1) if he reasonably believes—
(a) that there is an animal on the premises, and
(b) that the animal is one in relation to which the power under subsection (1) is exercisable.

(3) Subsection (2) does not authorise entry to any part of premises which is used as a private dwelling.

(4) Subject to subsection (5), a justice of the peace may, on the application of a constable, issue a warrant authorising a constable to enter and search premises, if necessary using reasonable force, for the purpose of exercising the power under subsection (1).

(5) The power to issue a warrant under subsection (4) is exercisable only if the justice of the peace is satisfied—
(a) that there are reasonable grounds for believing that there is on the premises an animal in relation to which an offence under section 8(1) or (2) has been committed, and
(b) that section 52 is satisfied in relation to the premises.

(6) In this section, references to an animal in relation to which an offence under section 8(1) or (2) has been committed include an animal which took part in an animal fight in relation to which such an offence was committed.

23 Entry and search under warrant in connection with offences

(1) Subject to subsection (2), a justice of the peace may, on the application of an inspector or constable, issue a warrant authorising an inspector or a constable to enter premises, if necessary using reasonable force, in order to search for evidence of the commission of a relevant offence.

(2) The power to issue a warrant under subsection (1) is exercisable only if the justice of the peace is satisfied—

(a) that there are reasonable grounds for believing—

(i) that a relevant offence has been committed on the premises, or

(ii) that evidence of the commission of a relevant offence is to be found on the premises, and

(b) that section 52 is satisfied in relation to the premises.

(3) In this section, "relevant offence" means an offence under any of sections 4 to 9, 13(6) and 34(9).

24 Entry for purposes of arrest

In section 17(1)(c) of the Police and Criminal Evidence Act 1984 (c. 60) (power of constable to enter and search premises for purpose of arresting a person for offence under specified enactments), at end insert—

"(v) any of sections 4, 5, 6(1) and (2), 7 and 8(1) and (2) of the Animal Welfare Act 2006 (offences relating to the prevention of harm to animals);".

25 Inspection of records required to be kept by holder of licence

(1) An inspector may require the holder of a licence to produce for inspection any records which he is required to keep by a condition of the licence.

(2) Where records which a person is so required to keep are stored in electronic form, the power under subsection (1) includes power to require the records to be made available for inspection—

(a) in a visible and legible form, or

(b) in a form from which they can readily be produced in a visible and legible form.

(3) An inspector may inspect and take copies of any records produced for inspection in pursuance of a requirement under this section.

26 Inspection in connection with licences

(1) An inspector may carry out an inspection in order to check compliance with—

(a) the conditions subject to which a licence is granted;

(b) provision made by or under this Act which is relevant to the carrying on of an activity to which a licence relates.

(2) An inspector may, for the purpose of carrying out an inspection under subsection (1), enter—

(a) premises specified in a licence as premises on which the carrying on of an activity is authorised;

(b) premises on which he reasonably believes an activity to which a licence relates is being carried on.

(3) Subsection (2) does not authorise entry to any part of premises which is used as a private dwelling unless 24 hours' notice of the intended entry is given to the occupier.

27 Inspection in connection with registration

(1) An inspector may carry out an inspection in order to check compliance with provision made by or under this Act which is relevant to the carrying on of an activity to which a registration for the purposes of section 13 relates.

(2) An inspector may, for the purpose of carrying out an inspection under subsection (1), enter premises on which he reasonably believes a person registered for the purposes of section 13 is carrying on an activity to which the registration relates.

(3) Subsection (2) does not authorise entry to any part of premises which is used as a private dwelling unless 24 hours' notice of the intended entry is given to the occupier.

28 Inspection of farm premises

(1) An inspector may carry out an inspection in order to—

(a) check compliance with regulations under section 12 which relate to animals bred or kept for farming purposes;

(b) ascertain whether any offence under or by virtue of this Act has been or is being committed in relation to such animals.

(2) An inspector may enter premises which he reasonably believes to be premises on which animals are bred or kept for farming purposes in order to carry out an inspection under subsection (1).

(3) Subsection (2) does not authorise entry to any part of premises which is used as a private dwelling.

(4) Subject to subsection (5), a justice of the peace may, on the application of an inspector, issue a warrant authorising an inspector to enter premises, if necessary using reasonable force, in order to carry out an inspection under subsection (1).

(5) The power to issue a warrant under subsection (4) is exercisable only if the justice of the peace is satisfied—

(a) that it is reasonable to carry out an inspection on the premises, and

(b) that section 52 is satisfied in relation to the premises.

29 Inspection relating to Community obligations

(1) An inspector may carry out an inspection in order to check compliance with regulations under section 12 which implement a Community obligation.

(2) An inspector may enter any premises in order to carry out an inspection under subsection (1).

(3) Subsection (2) does not authorise entry to any part of premises which is used as a private dwelling.

Prosecutions

30 Power of local authority to prosecute offences

A local authority in England or Wales may prosecute proceedings for any offence under this Act.

31 Time limits for prosecutions

(1) Notwithstanding anything in section 127(1) of the Magistrates' Courts Act 1980 (c. 43), a magistrates' court may try an information relating to an offence under this Act if the information is laid—

(a) before the end of the period of three years beginning with the date of the commission of the offence, and

(b) before the end of the period of six months beginning with the date on which evidence which the prosecutor thinks is sufficient to justify the proceedings comes to his knowledge.

(2) For the purposes of subsection (1)(b)—

(a) a certificate signed by or on behalf of the prosecutor and stating the date on which such evidence came to his knowledge shall be conclusive evidence of that fact, and

(b) a certificate stating that matter and purporting to be so signed shall be treated as so signed unless the contrary is proved.

Post-conviction powers

32 Imprisonment or fine

(1) A person guilty of an offence under any of sections 4, 5, 6(1) and (2), 7 and 8 shall be liable on summary conviction to—

(a) imprisonment for a term not exceeding 51 weeks, or

(b) a fine not exceeding £20,000,

or to both.

(2) A person guilty of an offence under section 9, 13(6) or 34(9) shall be liable on summary conviction to—

(a) imprisonment for a term not exceeding 51 weeks, or

(b) a fine not exceeding level 5 on the standard scale,

or to both.

(3) A person guilty of an offence under regulations under section 12 or 13 shall be liable on summary conviction to such penalty by way of imprisonment or fine as may be provided by regulations under that section.

(4) A person guilty of any other offence under this Act shall be liable on summary conviction to—

(a) imprisonment for a term not exceeding 51 weeks, or

(b) a fine not exceeding level 4 on the standard scale,

or to both.

(5) In relation to an offence committed before the commencement of section 281(5) of the Criminal Justice Act 2003 (c. 44), the reference in each of subsections (1)(a), (2)(a) and (4)(a) to 51 weeks is to be read as a reference to 6 months.

33 Deprivation

(1) If the person convicted of an offence under any of sections 4, 5, 6(1) and (2), 7, 8 and 9 is the owner of an animal in relation to which the offence was committed, the

court by or before which he is convicted may, instead of or in addition to dealing with him in any other way, make an order depriving him of ownership of the animal and for its disposal.

(2) Where the owner of an animal is convicted of an offence under section 34(9) because ownership of the animal is in breach of a disqualification under section 34(2), the court by or before which he is convicted may, instead of or in addition to dealing with him in any other way, make an order depriving him of ownership of the animal and for its disposal.

(3) Where the animal in respect of which an order under subsection (1) or (2) is made has any dependent offspring, the order may include provision depriving the person to whom it relates of ownership of the offspring and for its disposal.

(4) Where a court makes an order under subsection (1) or (2), it may—
   (a) appoint a person to carry out, or arrange for the carrying out of, the order;
   (b) require any person who has possession of an animal to which the order applies to deliver it up to enable the order to be carried out;
   (c) give directions with respect to the carrying out of the order;
   (d) confer additional powers (including power to enter premises where an animal to which the order applies is being kept) for the purpose of, or in connection with, the carrying out of the order;
   (e) order the offender to reimburse the expenses of carrying out the order.

(5) Directions under subsection (4)(c) may—
   (a) specify the manner in which an animal is to be disposed of, or
   (b) delegate the decision about the manner in which an animal is to be disposed of to a person appointed under subsection (4)(a).

(6) Where a court decides not to make an order under subsection (1) or (2) in relation to an offender, it shall—
   (a) give its reasons for the decision in open court, and
   (b) if it is a magistrates' court, cause them to be entered in the register of its proceedings.

(7) Subsection (6) does not apply where the court makes an order under section 34(1) in relation to the offender.

(8) In subsection (1), the reference to an animal in relation to which an offence was committed includes, in the case of an offence under section 8, an animal which took part in an animal fight in relation to which the offence was committed.

(9) In this section, references to disposing of an animal include destroying it.

34 Disqualification

(1) If a person is convicted of an offence to which this section applies, the court by or before which he is convicted may, instead of or in addition to dealing with him in any other way, make an order disqualifying him under any one or more of subsections (2) to (4) for such period as it thinks fit.

(2) Disqualification under this subsection disqualifies a person—
   (a) from owning animals,
   (b) from keeping animals,

(c) from participating in the keeping of animals, and
(d) from being party to an arrangement under which he is entitled to control or influence the way in which animals are kept.

(3) Disqualification under this subsection disqualifies a person from dealing in animals.

(4) Disqualification under this subsection disqualifies a person—
(a) from transporting animals, and
(b) from arranging for the transport of animals.

(5) Disqualification under subsection (2), (3) or (4) may be imposed in relation to animals generally, or in relation to animals of one or more kinds.

(6) The court by which an order under subsection (1) is made may specify a period during which the offender may not make an application under section 43(1) for termination of the order.

(7) The court by which an order under subsection (1) is made may—
(a) suspend the operation of the order pending an appeal, or
(b) where it appears to the court that the offender owns or keeps an animal to which the order applies, suspend the operation of the order, and of any order made under section 35 in connection with the disqualification, for such period as it thinks necessary for enabling alternative arrangements to be made in respect of the animal.

(8) Where a court decides not to make an order under subsection (1) in relation to an offender, it shall—
(a) give its reasons for the decision in open court, and
(b) if it is a magistrates' court, cause them to be entered in the register of its proceedings.

(9) A person who breaches a disqualification imposed by an order under subsection (1) commits an offence.

(10) This section applies to an offence under any of sections 4, 5, 6(1) and (2), 7, 8, 9 and 13(6) and subsection (9).

35 Seizure of animals in connection with disqualification

(1) Where—
(a) a court makes an order under section 34(1), and
(b) it appears to the court that the person to whom the order applies owns or keeps any animal contrary to the disqualification imposed by the order,

it may order that all animals he owns or keeps contrary to the disqualification be taken into possession.

(2) Where a person is convicted of an offence under section 34(9) because of owning or keeping an animal in breach of disqualification under section 34(2), the court by or before which he is convicted may order that all animals he owns or keeps in breach of the disqualification be taken into possession.

(3) An order under subsection (1) or (2), so far as relating to any animal owned by the person subject to disqualification, shall have effect as an order for the disposal of the animal.

(4) Any animal taken into possession in pursuance of an order under subsection (1) or (2) that is not owned by the person subject to disqualification shall be dealt with in such manner as the appropriate court may order.

(5) A court may not make an order for disposal under subsection (4) unless—

(a) it has given the owner of the animal an opportunity to be heard, or

(b) it is satisfied that it is not reasonably practicable to communicate with the owner.

(6) Where a court makes an order under subsection (4) for the disposal of an animal, the owner may—

(a) in the case of an order made by a magistrates' court, appeal against the order to the Crown Court;

(b) in the case of an order made by the Crown Court, appeal against the order to the Court of Appeal.

(7) In subsection (4), the reference to the appropriate court is to—

(a) the court which made the order under subsection (1) or (2), or

(b) in the case of an order made by a magistrates' court, to a magistrates' court for the same local justice area as that court.

(8) In this section, references to disposing of an animal include destroying it.

36 Section 35: supplementary

(1) The court by which an order under section 35 is made may—

(a) appoint a person to carry out, or arrange for the carrying out of, the order;

(b) require any person who has possession of an animal to which the order applies to deliver it up to enable the order to be carried out;

(c) give directions with respect to the carrying out of the order;

(d) confer additional powers (including power to enter premises where an animal to which the order applies is being kept) for the purpose of, or in connection with, the carrying out of the order;

(e) order the person subject to disqualification, or another person, to reimburse the expenses of carrying out the order.

(2) Directions under subsection (1)(c) may—

(a) specify the manner in which an animal is to be disposed of, or

(b) delegate the decision about the manner in which an animal is to be disposed of to a person appointed under subsection (1)(a).

(3) In determining how to exercise its powers under section 35 and this section, the court shall have regard, amongst other things, to—

(a) the desirability of protecting the value of any animal to which the order applies, and

(b) the desirability of avoiding increasing any expenses which a person may be ordered to reimburse.

(4) In determining how to exercise a power delegated under subsection (2)(b), a person shall have regard, amongst other things, to the things mentioned in subsection (3)(a) and (b).

(5) If the owner of an animal ordered to be disposed of under section 35 is subject to a liability by virtue of subsection (1)(e), any amount to which he is entitled as a result of sale of the animal may be reduced by an amount equal to that liability.

37 Destruction in the interests of the animal

(1) The court by or before which a person is convicted of an offence under any of sections 4, 5, 6(1) and (2), 7, 8(1) and (2) and 9 may order the destruction of an animal in relation to which the offence was committed if it is satisfied, on the basis of evidence given by a veterinary surgeon, that it is appropriate to do so in the interests of the animal.

(2) A court may not make an order under subsection (1) unless—

- (a) it has given the owner of the animal an opportunity to be heard, or
- (b) it is satisfied that it is not reasonably practicable to communicate with the owner.

(3) Where a court makes an order under subsection (1), it may—

- (a) appoint a person to carry out, or arrange for the carrying out of, the order;
- (b) require a person who has possession of the animal to deliver it up to enable the order to be carried out;
- (c) give directions with respect to the carrying out of the order (including directions about how the animal is to be dealt with until it is destroyed);
- (d) confer additional powers (including power to enter premises where the animal is being kept) for the purpose of, or in connection with, the carrying out of the order;
- (e) order the offender or another person to reimburse the expenses of carrying out the order.

(4) Where a court makes an order under subsection (1), each of the offender and, if different, the owner of the animal may—

- (a) in the case of an order made by a magistrates' court, appeal against the order to the Crown Court;
- (b) in the case of an order made by the Crown Court, appeal against the order to the Court of Appeal.

(5) Subsection (4) does not apply if the court by which the order is made directs that it is appropriate in the interests of the animal that the carrying out of the order should not be delayed.

(6) In subsection (1), the reference to an animal in relation to which an offence was committed includes, in the case of an offence under section 8(1) or (2), an animal which took part in an animal fight in relation to which the offence was committed.

38 Destruction of animals involved in fighting offences

(1) The court by or before which a person is convicted of an offence under section 8(1) or (2) may order the destruction of an animal in relation to which the offence was committed on grounds other than the interests of the animal.

(2) A court may not make an order under subsection (1) unless—

- (a) it has given the owner of the animal an opportunity to be heard, or

(b) it is satisfied that it is not reasonably practicable to communicate with the owner.

(3) Where a court makes an order under subsection (1), it may—

(a) appoint a person to carry out, or arrange for the carrying out of, the order;

(b) require a person who has possession of the animal to deliver it up to enable the order to be carried out;

(c) give directions with respect to the carrying out of the order (including directions about how the animal is to be dealt with until it is destroyed);

(d) confer additional powers (including power to enter premises where the animal is being kept) for the purpose of, or in connection with, the carrying out of the order;

(e) order the offender or another person to reimburse the expenses of carrying out the order.

(4) Where a court makes an order under subsection (1) in relation to an animal which is owned by a person other than the offender, that person may—

(a) in the case of an order made by a magistrates' court, appeal against the order to the Crown Court;

(b) in the case of an order made by the Crown Court, appeal against the order to the Court of Appeal.

(5) In subsection (1), the reference to an animal in relation to which the offence was committed includes an animal which took part in an animal fight in relation to which the offence was committed.

39 Reimbursement of expenses relating to animals involved in fighting offences

(1) The court by or before which a person is convicted of an offence under section 8(1) or (2) may order the offender or another person to reimburse any expenses incurred by the police in connection with the keeping of an animal in relation to which the offence was committed.

(2) In subsection (1), the reference to an animal in relation to which the offence was committed includes an animal which took part in a fight in relation to which the offence was committed.

40 Forfeiture of equipment used in offences

(1) Where a person is convicted of an offence under any of sections 4, 5, 6(1) and (2), 7 and 8, the court by or before which he is convicted may order any qualifying item which is shown to the satisfaction of the court to relate to the offence to be—

(a) forfeited, and

(b) destroyed or dealt with in such manner as may be specified in the order.

(2) The reference in subsection (1) to any qualifying item is—

(a) in the case of a conviction for an offence under section 4, to anything designed or adapted for causing suffering to an animal;

(b) in the case of a conviction for an offence under section 5, to anything designed or adapted for carrying out a prohibited procedure on an animal;

(c) in the case of a conviction for an offence under section 6(1) or (2), to anything designed or adapted for removing the whole or any part of a dog's tail;

(d) in the case of a conviction for an offence under section 7, to anything designed or adapted for administering any drug or substance to an animal;

(e) in the case of a conviction for an offence under section 8(1) or (2), to anything designed or adapted for use in connection with an animal fight;

(f) in the case of a conviction for an offence under section 8(3), to a video recording of an animal fight, including anything on or in which the recording is kept.

(3) The court shall not order anything to be forfeited under subsection (1) if a person claiming to be the owner of it or otherwise interested in it applies to be heard by the court, unless he has been given an opportunity to show cause why the order should not be made.

(4) An expression used in any of paragraphs (a) to (f) of subsection (2) has the same meaning as in the provision referred to in that paragraph.

41 Orders under section 33, 35, 37, 38 or 40: pending appeals

(1) Nothing may be done under an order under section 33, 35, 37 or 38 with respect to an animal or an order under section 40 unless—

(a) the period for giving notice of appeal against the order has expired,

(b) the period for giving notice of appeal against the conviction on which the order was made has expired, and

(c) if the order or conviction is the subject of an appeal, the appeal has been determined or withdrawn.

(2) Subsection (1) does not apply to an order under section 37(1) if the order is the subject of a direction under subsection (5) of that section.

(3) Where the effect of an order is suspended under subsection (1)—

(a) no requirement imposed or directions given in connection with the order shall have effect, but

(b) the court may give directions about how any animal to which the order applies is to be dealt with during the suspension.

(4) Directions under subsection (3)(b) may, in particular—

(a) authorise the animal to be taken into possession;

(b) authorise the removal of the animal to a place of safety;

(c) authorise the animal to be cared for either on the premises where it was being kept when it was taken into possession or at some other place;

(d) appoint a person to carry out, or arrange for the carrying out, of the directions;

(e) require any person who has possession of the animal to deliver it up for the purposes of the directions;

(f) confer additional powers (including power to enter premises where the animal is being kept) for the purpose of, or in connection with, the carrying out of the directions;

(g) provide for the recovery of any expenses in relation to removal or care of the animal which are incurred in carrying out the directions.

(5) Any expenses a person is directed to pay under subsection (4)(g) shall be recoverable summarily as a civil debt.

(6) Where the effect of an order under section 33 is suspended under subsection (1) the person to whom the order relates may not sell or part with any animal to which the order applies.

(7) Failure to comply with subsection (6) is an offence.

42 Orders with respect to licences

(1) If a person is convicted of an offence under any of sections 4, 5, 6(1) and (2), 7 to 9, 11 and 13(6), the court by or before which he is convicted may, instead of or in addition to dealing with him in any other way—

(a) make an order cancelling any licence held by him;

(b) make an order disqualifying him, for such period as it thinks fit, from holding a licence.

(2) Disqualification under subsection (1)(b) may be imposed in relation to licences generally or in relation to licences of one or more kinds.

(3) The court by which an order under subsection (1)(b) is made may specify a period during which the offender may not make an application under section 43(1) for termination of the order.

(4) The court by which an order under subsection (1) is made may suspend the operation of the order pending an appeal.

43 Termination of disqualification under section 34 or 42

(1) A person who is disqualified by virtue of an order under section 34 or 42 may apply to the appropriate court for the termination of the order.

(2) No application under subsection (1) may be made—

(a) before the end of the period of one year beginning with the date on which the order is made,

(b) where a previous application under that subsection has been made in relation to the same order, before the end of the period of one year beginning with the date on which the previous application was determined, or

(c) before the end of any period specified under section 34(6), 42(3) or subsection (5) below in relation to the order.

(3) On an application under subsection (1), the court may—

(a) terminate the disqualification,

(b) vary the disqualification so as to make it less onerous, or

(c) refuse the application.

(4) When determining an application under subsection (1), the court shall have regard to the character of the applicant, his conduct since the imposition of the disqualification and any other circumstances of the case.

(5) Where the court refuses an application under subsection (1), it may specify a period during which the applicant may not make a further application under that subsection in relation to the order concerned.

(6) The court may order an applicant under subsection (1) to pay all or part of the costs of the application.

(7) In subsection (1), the reference to the appropriate court is to—

(a) the court which made the order under section 34 or 42, or

(b) in the case of an order made by a magistrates' court, to a magistrates' court acting for the same local justice area as that court.

44 Orders made on conviction for reimbursement of expenses

Where an order is made under section 33(4)(e), 36(1)(e), 37(3)(e), 38(3)(e) or 39(1), the expenses that are required by the order to be reimbursed shall not be regarded for the purposes of the Magistrates' Courts Act 1980 (c. 43) as a sum adjudged to be paid by a summary conviction, but shall be recoverable summarily as a civil debt.

45 Orders for reimbursement of expenses: right of appeal for non-offenders

(1) Where a court makes an order to which this section applies, the person against whom the order is made may—

(a) in the case of an order made by a magistrates' court, appeal against the order to the Crown Court;

(b) in the case of an order made by the Crown Court, appeal against the order to the Court of Appeal.

(2) This section applies to—

(a) an order under section 36(1)(e) against a person other than the person subject to disqualification, and

(b) an order under section 37(3)(e), 38(3)(e) or 39(1) against a person other than the offender.

Scotland

46 Effect in Scotland of disqualification under section 34

(1) Disqualification by virtue of an order under section 34(1) has effect in relation to Scotland.

(2) A person who breaches a disqualification under section 34 commits an offence.

(3) A person guilty of an offence under subsection (2) is liable on summary conviction to—

(a) imprisonment for a term not exceeding 6 months, or

(b) a fine not exceeding level 5 on the standard scale,

or to both.

47 Deprivation orders in connection with offence under section 46(2)

(1) Where a person is convicted of an offence under section 46(2) because of owning or keeping an animal in breach of disqualification under section 34(2), the convicting court may make an order (in this section and sections 49 and 50 referred to as a

"deprivation order") in respect of any animal in relation to which the offence was committed.

(2) A deprivation order is an order—
 (a) depriving a person of possession or ownership (or both) of an animal, and
 (b) for—
  (i) the destruction,
  (ii) the sale, or
  (iii) another disposal,
 of the animal.

(3) Where the court decides not to make a deprivation order, it must state its reasons.

(4) A deprivation order may be made in addition to, or instead of, any other penalty or order which may be imposed in relation to the offence.

(5) A deprivation order may make provision in respect of any dependent offspring of an animal to which it applies.

(6) A deprivation order may include—
 (a) provision—
  (i) appointing a person who is to secure that the order is carried out,
  (ii) requiring any person possessing an animal to which the order applies to give it up to a person appointed under sub-paragraph (i),
 (b) provision authorising—
  (i) a person appointed under paragraph (a)(i), and
  (ii) any person acting on that person's behalf,
 to enter, for the purposes of securing that the order is carried out, any premises where an animal to which the order applies is kept,
 (c) such other provisions as the court considers appropriate in connection with the order.

(7) Provision under subsection (6)(c) may, in particular—
 (a) require reimbursement of any expenses reasonably incurred in carrying out the order,
 (b) relate to the retention of any proceeds of the disposal.

(8) The court may not make a deprivation order which involves the destruction of an animal unless it is satisfied, on evidence provided (orally or in writing) by a veterinary surgeon, that destruction would be in the interests of the animal.

(9) Before making a deprivation order, the court must give the owner of the animal concerned an opportunity to make representations unless it is not practicable for it to do so.

48 Seizure orders where disqualification breached: Scotland

(1) Where the court is satisfied that a person who is subject to disqualification under section 34 owns or keeps an animal in breach of the disqualification, the court may make an order (in this section and sections 49 and 50 referred to as a "seizure order") in respect of all animals which the person owns or keeps in breach of the disqualification.

(2) A seizure order may be made—

(a) on summary application by an inspector,

(b) even if proceedings have not been, or are not likely to be, taken against the person for an offence under section 46(2).

(3) A seizure order is an order—

(a) depriving a person of possession or ownership (or both) of an animal, and

(b) for—

(i) the destruction,

(ii) the sale, or

(iii) another disposal,

of the animal.

(4) A seizure order may include—

(a) provision—

(i) appointing a person who is to secure that the order is carried out,

(ii) requiring any person possessing an animal to which the order applies to give it up to a person appointed under sub-paragraph (i),

(b) provision authorising—

(i) a person appointed under paragraph (a)(i), and

(ii) any person acting on that person's behalf,

to enter, for the purposes of securing that the order is carried out, any premises where an animal to which the order applies is kept,

(c) such other provision as the court considers appropriate in connection with the order.

(5) Provision under subsection (4)(c) may, in particular—

(a) require reimbursement of any expenses reasonably incurred in carrying out the order,

(b) relate to the retention of any proceeds of the disposal.

(6) The court may not make a seizure order which involves the destruction of an animal unless it is satisfied, on evidence provided (orally or in writing) by a veterinary surgeon, that destruction would be in the interests of the animal.

(7) Before making a seizure order, the court must give the owner of the animals concerned an opportunity to make representations unless it is not practicable for it to do so.

(8) In determining whether or how to make a seizure order, the court must have regard to the desirability of—

(a) protecting the value of any animal to which the order applies, and

(b) avoiding increasing any expenses which a person may be required to reimburse.

(9) When an application is made under subsection (2)(a), the court may make an order under this subsection (an "interim order") containing such provision as the court considers appropriate in relation to the keeping of an animal until the application is finally determined.

(10) Subsections (4), (5)(a) and (8) apply in relation to an interim order as they apply in relation to a seizure order.

(11) In subsection (2)(a), an "inspector" is a person—

(a) appointed as inspector by the Scottish Ministers, or authorised by them, for the purposes of this section, or

(b) appointed as inspector by a local authority for the purposes of this section.

(12) In subsection (11)(b), a "local authority" means a council constituted under section 2 of the Local Government etc. (Scotland) Act 1994 (c. 39).

49 Appeals against deprivation orders and seizure orders

(1) Any deprivation order is, for the purposes of any appeal under the Criminal Procedure (Scotland) Act 1995 (c. 46), to be treated as a sentence.

(2) Where a deprivation order is made, any person (apart from a person who may appeal against the order by virtue of subsection (1)) who has an interest in any animal to which the order applies may appeal to the High Court of Justiciary against the order by the same procedure as applies under subsection (1) in relation to a deprivation order.

(3) The disqualified person by reference to whom a seizure order is made, or any person (apart from that disqualified person) who entered the process prior to the making of the order, may appeal to the sheriff principal against the order.

(4) The operation of any deprivation order or seizure order is suspended until—

(a) any period for an appeal against the order has expired,

(b) the period for an appeal against the conviction on which the order depends has expired, and

(c) any appeal against the order or that conviction has been withdrawn or finally determined.

(5) Where the operation of a deprivation order or seizure order is suspended under subsection (4), or such an order is not executable because decree has not been extracted, the court which made the order may make an order under this subsection (an "interim order") containing such provisions as the court considers appropriate in relation to the keeping of an animal for so long as the first-mentioned order remains suspended or inexecutable.

(6) An interim order may, in particular—

(a) make provision—

(i) appointing a person who is to secure that the order is carried out,

(ii) requiring any person possessing an animal to which the order applies to give it up to a person appointed under sub-paragraph (i),

(b) make provision authorising—

(i) a person appointed under paragraph (a)(i), and

(ii) any person acting on that person's behalf,

to enter, for the purposes of securing that the order is carried out, any premises where an animal to which the order applies is kept,

(c) for reimbursement of any expenses reasonably incurred in carrying out the order.

(7) In determining whether or how to make an interim order, the court must have regard to the desirability of—

(a) protecting the value of any animal to which the order applies, and

(b) avoiding increasing any expenses which a person may be required to reimburse.

50 Deprivation orders, seizure orders and interim orders: offences

(1) Where the operation of a deprivation order is suspended under section 49(4), a person commits an offence if the person sells or otherwise parts with an animal to which the order applies.

(2) A person commits an offence if the person intentionally obstructs a person in the carrying out of—

(a) a deprivation order,

(b) a seizure order,

(c) an interim order under section 48(9) or 49(5).

(3) A person guilty of an offence under subsection (1) or (2) is liable on summary conviction to—

(a) imprisonment for a term not exceeding 6 months, or

(b) a fine not exceeding level 5 on the standard scale,

or to both.

General

51 Inspectors

(1) In this Act, "inspector", in the context of any provision, means a person appointed to be an inspector for the purposes of that provision by—

(a) the appropriate national authority, or

(b) a local authority.

(2) In appointing a person to be an inspector for purposes of this Act, a local authority shall have regard to guidance issued by the appropriate national authority.

(3) The appropriate national authority may, in connection with guidance under subsection (2), draw up a list of persons whom the authority considers suitable for appointment by a local authority to be an inspector for purposes of this Act.

(4) A person may be included in a list under subsection (3) as suitable for appointment as an inspector for all the purposes of this Act or only for such one or more of those purposes as may be specified in the list.

(5) An inspector shall not be liable in any civil or criminal proceedings for anything done in the purported performance of his functions under this Act if the court is satisfied that the act was done in good faith and that there were reasonable grounds for doing it.

(6) Relief from liability of an inspector under subsection (5) shall not affect any liability of any other person in respect of the inspector's act.

52 Conditions for grant of warrant

(1) This section is satisfied in relation to premises if any of the following four conditions is met.

(2) The first condition is that the whole of the premises is used as a private dwelling and the occupier has been informed of the decision to apply for a warrant.

(3) The second condition is that any part of the premises is not used as a private dwelling and that each of the following applies to the occupier of the premises—

(a) he has been informed of the decision to seek entry to the premises and of the reasons for that decision;

(b) he has failed to allow entry to the premises on being requested to do so by an inspector or a constable;

(c) he has been informed of the decision to apply for a warrant.

(4) The third condition is that—

(a) the premises are unoccupied or the occupier is absent, and

(b) notice of intention to apply for a warrant has been left in a conspicuous place on the premises.

(5) The fourth condition is that it is inappropriate to inform the occupier of the decision to apply for a warrant because—

(a) it would defeat the object of entering the premises, or

(b) entry is required as a matter of urgency.

53 Powers of entry, inspection and search: supplementary

Schedule 2 (which makes supplementary provision in relation to powers of entry, inspection and search) has effect.

54 Power to stop and detain vehicles

(1) A constable in uniform or, if accompanied by such a constable, an inspector may stop and detain a vehicle for the purpose of entering and searching it in the exercise of a power conferred—

(a) by section 19(1), or

(b) by a warrant under section 19(4) or 23(1).

(2) A constable in uniform may stop and detain a vehicle for the purpose of entering and searching it in the exercise of a power conferred—

(a) by section 22(2), or

(b) by a warrant under section 22(4).

(3) If accompanied by a constable in uniform, an inspector may stop and detain a vehicle for the purpose of entering it and carrying out an inspection in the exercise of a power conferred—

(a) by section 26(2), 27(2), 28(2) or 29(2), or

(b) by a warrant under section 28(4).

(4) A vehicle may be detained for as long as is reasonably required to permit a search or inspection to be carried out (including the exercise of any related power under this Act) either at the place where the vehicle was first detained or nearby.

55 Power to detain vessels, aircraft and hovercraft

(1) Where an inspector appointed by the appropriate national authority certifies in writing that he is satisfied that an offence under or by virtue of this Act is being or has been committed on board a vessel in port, the vessel may be detained.

(2) A certificate under subsection (1) shall—

(a) specify each offence to which it relates, and

(b) set out the inspector's reasons for being satisfied that each offence to which it relates is being or has been committed.

(3) Section 284 of the Merchant Shipping Act 1995 (c. 21) (which provides for enforcement of the detention of a ship under that Act by specified officers) shall apply as if the power of detention under subsection (1) were conferred by that Act.

(4) An officer who detains a vessel in reliance on a certificate under subsection (1) shall as soon as is reasonably practicable give a copy of it to the master or person in charge of the vessel.

(5) A vessel may be detained under subsection (1) until the appropriate national authority otherwise directs.

(6) The appropriate national authority may by regulations—

(a) apply this section to aircraft or hovercraft, with such modifications as the authority thinks fit, or

(b) make such other provision for the detention of aircraft or hovercraft in relation to offences under or by virtue of this Act as the authority thinks fit.

56 Obtaining of documents in connection with carrying out orders etc.

(1) Where—

(a) an order under section 20(1), 33(1) or (2), 35(1) or (2) or 37(1) has effect, and

(b) the owner of an animal to which the order relates has in his possession, or under his control, documents which are relevant to the carrying out of the order or any directions given in connection with it,

the owner shall, if so required by a person authorised to carry out the order, deliver the documents to that person as soon as practicable and in any event before the end of the period of 10 days beginning with the date on which he is notified of the requirement.

(2) Where—

(a) directions under section 41(3)(b) have effect, and

(b) the owner of an animal to which the directions relate has in his possession, or under his control, documents which are relevant to the carrying out of the directions,

the owner shall, if so required by a person authorised to carry out the directions, deliver the documents to that person as soon as practicable and in any event before the end of the period of 10 days beginning with the date on which he is notified of the requirement.

(3) A person who fails without reasonable excuse to comply with subsection (1) or (2) commits an offence.

57 Offences by bodies corporate

(1) Where an offence under this Act is committed by a body corporate and is proved to have been committed with the consent or connivance of or to be attributable to any neglect on the part of—

(a) any director, manager, secretary or other similar officer of the body corporate, or

(b) any person who was purporting to act in any such capacity,

he (as well as the body corporate) commits the offence and shall be liable to be proceeded against and punished accordingly.

(2) Where the affairs of a body corporate are managed by its members, subsection (1) applies in relation to the acts and defaults of a member in connection with his functions of management as if he were a director of the body corporate.

58 Scientific research

(1) Nothing in this Act applies to anything lawfully done under the Animals (Scientific Procedures) Act 1986 (c. 14).

(2) No power of entry, inspection or search conferred by or under this Act, except for any such power conferred by section 28, may be exercised in relation to a place which is—

(a) designated under section 6 of the Animals (Scientific Procedures) Act 1986 as a scientific procedure establishment, or

(b) designated under section 7 of that Act as a breeding establishment or as a supplying establishment.

(3) Section 9 does not apply in relation to an animal which—

(a) is being kept, at a place designated under section 6 of the Animals (Scientific Procedures) Act 1986 as a scientific procedure establishment, for use in regulated procedures,

(b) is being kept, at a place designated under section 7 of that Act as a breeding establishment, for use for breeding animals for use in regulated procedures,

(c) is being kept at such a place, having been bred there for use in regulated procedures, or

(d) is being kept, at a place designated under section 7 of that Act as a supplying establishment, for the purpose of being supplied for use elsewhere in regulated procedures.

(4) In subsection (3), "regulated procedure" has the same meaning as in the Animals (Scientific Procedures) Act 1986.

59 Fishing

Nothing in this Act applies in relation to anything which occurs in the normal course of fishing.

60 Crown application

(1) Subject to the provisions of this section, this Act and regulations and orders made under it shall bind the Crown.

(2) No contravention by the Crown of any provision made by or under this Act shall make the Crown criminally liable; but the High Court may declare unlawful any act or omission of the Crown which constitutes such a contravention.

(3) Notwithstanding subsection (2), the provisions of this Act and of regulations and orders made under it shall apply to persons in the service of the Crown as they apply to other persons.

(4) If the Secretary of State certifies that it appears to him appropriate in the interests of national security that powers of entry conferred by or under this Act should not be exercisable in relation to Crown premises specified in the certificate, those powers shall not be exercisable in relation to those premises.

(5) In subsection (4), "Crown premises" means premises held, or used, by or on behalf of the Crown.

(6) No power of entry conferred by or under this Act may be exercised in relation to land belonging to Her Majesty in right of Her private estates.

(7) In subsection (6), the reference to Her Majesty's private estates shall be construed in accordance with section 1 of the Crown Private Estates Act 1862 (c. 37).

61 Orders and regulations

(1) Any power of the Secretary of State, the National Assembly for Wales or the Scottish Ministers to make orders or regulations under this Act, except the power under section 17(1) of the National Assembly for Wales, is exercisable by statutory instrument.

(2) No regulations under section 1(3), 5(4), 6, 12 or 13 shall be made by the Secretary of State unless a draft of the instrument containing the regulations has been laid before, and approved by a resolution of, each House of Parliament.

(3) No order under section 17(1) shall be made by the Secretary of State unless a draft of the instrument containing the order has been laid before Parliament.

(4) Subsection (3) does not apply in relation to an order revoking a code of practice in connection with its replacement by a new one.

(5) A statutory instrument containing regulations under section 55(6) made by the Secretary of State shall be subject to annulment in pursuance of a resolution of either House of Parliament.

62 General interpretation

(1) In this Act—

"animal" has the meaning given by section 1(1);

"appropriate national authority" means—

(a) in relation to England, the Secretary of State;

(b) in relation to Wales, the National Assembly for Wales;

"enactment" includes an enactment contained in subordinate legislation (within the meaning of the Interpretation Act 1978 (c. 30));

"licence" means a licence for the purposes of section 13;

"local authority" means—

(a) in relation to England, a county council, a district council, a London borough council, the Common Council of the City of London or the Council of the Isles of Scilly;

(b) in relation to Wales, a county council or a county borough council;

"premises" includes any place and, in particular, includes—

(a) any vehicle, vessel, aircraft or hovercraft;

(b) any tent or movable structure;

"protected animal" has the meaning given by section 2;

""suffering" means physical or mental suffering and related expressions shall be construed accordingly;

"veterinary surgeon" means a person registered in the register of veterinary surgeons, or the supplementary veterinary register, kept under the Veterinary Surgeons Act 1966 (c. 36).

(2) In this Act, references to the occupier of premises, in relation to any vehicle, vessel, aircraft or hovercraft, are to the person who appears to be in charge of the vehicle, vessel, aircraft or hovercraft, and "unoccupied" shall be construed accordingly.

(3) In this Act, references to a part of premises which is used as a private dwelling include any yard, garden, garage or outhouse which is used for purposes in connection with it.

(4) In this Act, references to responsibility, in relation to an animal, are to be read in accordance with section 3.

(5) In this Act, references to the needs of an animal are to be read in accordance with section 9(2).

(6) In this Act, references to a "relevant post-conviction power" are to a power conferred by—

(a) section 33, 34, 37 or 42 of this Act,

(b) section 4(2) of the Performing Animals (Regulation) Act 1925 (c. 38) (power to remove name from register under Act and disqualify from registration),

(c) section 5(3) of the Pet Animals Act 1951 (c. 35) (power to cancel licence under Act and disqualify from carrying on licensable activity),

(d) section 3(3) of the Animal Boarding Establishments Act 1963 (c. 43) (provision corresponding to that mentioned in paragraph (c) above),

(e) section 4(3) of the Riding Establishments Act 1964 (c. 70) (further corresponding provision),

(f) section 3(4) of the Guard Dogs Act 1975 (c. 50) (power to cancel licence under Act),

(g) section 6(2) of the Dangerous Wild Animals Act 1976 (c. 38) (power to cancel licence under Act and disqualify from carrying on licensable activity), or

(h) section 4(4) of the Zoo Licensing Act 1981 (c. 37) (power to refuse licence under Act for conviction for an offence).

63 Financial provisions

(1) There shall be paid out of money provided by Parliament—

(a) any expenditure under this Act of the Secretary of State, and

(b) any increase attributable to this Act in the sums payable out of money so provided under any other enactment.

(2) There shall be paid into the Consolidated Fund any increase attributable to this Act in the sums payable into that Fund under any other enactment.

64 Minor and consequential amendments

Schedule 3 (minor and consequential amendments) has effect.

65 Repeals

The enactments specified in Schedule 4 are hereby repealed to the extent specified.

66 Transition

(1) Each of the Secretary of State, the National Assembly for Wales and the Scottish Ministers may by order make such transitional provision or savings as are considered necessary or expedient in connection with the coming into force of any provision of this Act.

(2) Power under subsection (1) includes power to make different provision for different cases.

(3) Section 34(9) shall apply in relation to a disqualification imposed by an order under section 1 of the Protection of Animals (Amendment) Act 1954 (c. 40) (power to disqualify persons convicted of cruelty to animals) as it applies in relation to a disqualification imposed by an order under section 34(1).

(4) In relation to a person convicted of an offence under section 34(9) by virtue of breaching a disqualification imposed by an order under section 1 of the Protection of Animals (Amendment) Act 1954, section 35(2) shall have effect with the substitution for the words from "owning" to "keeps" of "having custody of an animal in breach of disqualification under section 1 of the Protection of Animals (Amendment) Act 1954, the court by or before which he is convicted may order that all animals of which he has custody".

(5) Section 43 shall apply in relation to a person who is disqualified by virtue of an order under section 1 of the Protection of Animals (Amendment) Act 1954 as it applies in relation to a person who is disqualified by virtue of an order under section 34 or 42.

(6) In its application by virtue of subsection (5), section 43(2)(c) shall have effect with the omission of the words "section 34(6), 42(3) or".

67 Extent

(1) Subject to the following provisions, this Act extends to England and Wales only.

(2) Sections 46 to 50 and 68(2) extend to Scotland only.

(3) The following provisions also extend to Scotland—
- (a) sections 57 and 60(1) and (4) to (7), so far as relating to sections 46 to 50,
- (b) section 61(1), so far as relating to sections 66 and 68,
- (c) section 66(1) and (2), this section and sections 68(1), (3) and (4) and 69,
- (d) paragraphs 2, 12 and 14 of Schedule 3, and section 64 so far as relating to them, and

(e) such of the repeals in Schedule 4 as are mentioned in subsection (4), and section 65 so far as relating to them.

(4) The repeals referred to are—

(a) in section 1(3) of the Protection of Animals Act 1934 (c. 21), the provision about the meaning of "horse" and "bull";

(b) in the Protection of Animals (Amendment) Act 1954 (c. 40)—

(i) in section 1(1), the words "the Protection of Animals Act 1911 or", and

(ii) in section 4(1)(a), the words from ", in relation to England" to "in relation to Scotland,";

(c) in the Protection of Animals (Anaesthetics) Act 1954 (c. 46), section 2(2) and Part 1 of Schedule 2;

(d) in the Abandonment of Animals Act 1960 (c. 43)—

(i) section 2(a), and

(ii) in section 3(2), the words "the Protection of Animals Acts 1911 to 1960, or" and the words ", as the case may be";

(e) in section 4(2) of the Animals (Cruel Poisons) Act 1962 (c. 26), the words from "and the Protection of Animals Acts 1911" to "and this Act";

(f) in the Protection of Animals (Anaesthetics) Act 1964 (c. 39), section 2(1)(a);

(g) in the Agriculture (Miscellaneous Provisions) Act 1968 (c. 34)—

(i) section 7(3), and

(ii) in section 8(5), the words "the Protection of Animals Acts 1911 to 1964 or".

(5) The following provisions also extend to Northern Ireland—

(a) section 61(1), so far as relating to sections 66 and 68,

(b) section 66(1) and (2), this section and sections 68(1), (3) and (4) and 69, and

(c) paragraphs 12 and 14 of Schedule 3, and section 64 so far as relating to them.

68 Commencement

(1) This section and sections 61, 67 and 69 shall come into force on the day on which this Act is passed.

(2) Sections 46 to 50 shall come into force on such day as the Scottish Ministers may by order appoint.

(3) The remaining provisions of this Act—

(a) so far as relating to England, Scotland or Northern Ireland, shall come into force on such day as the Secretary of State may by order appoint, and

(b) so far as relating to Wales, shall come into force on such day as the National Assembly for Wales may by order appoint.

(4) Power under subsection (3) includes power to appoint different days for different purposes.

69 Short title

This Act may be cited as the Animal Welfare Act 2006.

SCHEDULES

SCHEDULE 1

Section 13

REGULATIONS UNDER SECTION 13

PART 1

LICENCES FOR THE PURPOSES OF THE SECTION

Introductory

1 This Part has effect in relation to regulations under section 13(7) about licences for the purposes of section 13.

Licensing authority

2 Regulations shall provide for the licensing authority to be—

(a) a local authority, or

(b) the appropriate national authority.

3 Where the licensing authority is a local authority, regulations may require the licensing authority to have regard in carrying out its functions under the regulations to such guidance as may be issued by the appropriate national authority.

Period of licence

4 Regulations may, in particular—

(a) make provision about the period for which licences are to be granted;

(b) make provision, in connection with the death of the holder of a licence, for the continuation in force of the licence for such period and subject to such conditions as the regulations may provide.

5 Regulations may not provide for licences to be granted for a period of more than 3 years.

Exercise of licensing functions

6 Regulations may, in particular—

(a) require a licensing authority not to grant a licence unless satisfied as to a matter specified in the regulations;

(b) require a licensing authority to have regard, in deciding whether to grant a licence, to a matter specified in the regulations.

7 Regulations shall make provision requiring a licensing authority not to grant a licence authorising the carrying on of an activity on specific premises unless the premises have been inspected as the regulations may provide.

Grant of licence subject to conditions

8 (1) Regulations may, in particular, make provision for the grant of a licence subject to conditions.

(2) Provision of the kind mentioned in sub-paragraph (1) may—

(a) enable a licensing authority to attach conditions to a licence;

(b) require a licensing authority to attach to a licence conditions specified in the regulations.

Breach of licence condition

9 (1) Regulations may provide for breach of a condition of a licence to be an offence.

(2) Regulations may not provide for an offence of breach of condition of a licence to be triable on indictment or punishable with—

(a) imprisonment for a term exceeding 51 weeks, or

(b) a fine exceeding level 5 on the standard scale.

(3) Regulations may provide that an offence of breach of condition of a licence is to be treated as a relevant offence for the purposes of section 23.

(4) Regulations may apply a relevant post-conviction power in relation to conviction for an offence of breach of condition of a licence.

Appeals

10 Regulations may, in particular, make provision for appeals in relation to decisions of a licensing authority under the regulations.

Fees

11 Regulations may include provision for fees or other charges in relation to the carrying out of functions of the licensing authority under the regulations.

PART 2

REGISTRATION FOR THE PURPOSES OF THE SECTION

Introductory

12 This Part has effect in relation to regulations under section 13(7) about registration for the purposes of section 13.

Registering authority

13 Regulations shall provide for the registering authority to be—

(a) a local authority, or

(b) the appropriate national authority.

14 Where the registering authority is a local authority, regulations may require the registering authority to have regard in carrying out its functions under the regulations to such guidance as may be issued by the appropriate national authority.

Exercise of registration functions

15 Regulations may, in particular—

(a) require a registering authority not to register an applicant for registration unless satisfied as to a matter specified in the regulations;

(b) require a registering authority to have regard, in deciding whether to register an applicant for registration, to a matter specified in the regulations.

Appeals

16 Regulations may, in particular, make provision for appeals in relation to decisions of a registering authority under the regulations.

Fees

17 Regulations may include provision for fees or other charges in relation to the carrying out of functions of the registering authority under the regulations.

PART 3

SUPPLEMENTARY

18 Power to make regulations under section 13(7) includes power—

(a) to make provision for purposes other than the purpose of promoting the welfare of animals for which a person is responsible;

(b) to make different provision for different cases or areas;

(c) to provide for exemptions from a provision of the regulations, either subject to specified conditions or without conditions.

19 (1) Power to make regulations under section 13 includes power to make incidental, supplementary, consequential or transitional provision or savings.

(2) In the case of provision consequential on the repeal of an enactment specified in section 13(8), the power under sub-paragraph (1) includes power—

(a) to amend or repeal an enactment;

(b) to make provision for the purpose of continuing the effect of an enactment repealed under paragraph (a).

(3) The power under sub-paragraph (2)(b) includes power to provide that breach of a provision of the regulations is an offence, but does not include power to create an offence triable on indictment or punishable with—

(a) imprisonment for a term exceeding 51 weeks, or

(b) a fine exceeding level 5 on the standard scale.

SCHEDULE 2

Section 53

POWERS OF ENTRY, INSPECTION AND SEARCH: SUPPLEMENTARY

Safeguards etc. in connection with powers of entry conferred by warrant

1 (1) Sections 15 and 16 of the Police and Criminal Evidence Act 1984 (c. 60) shall have effect in relation to the issue of a warrant under section 19(4) or 23(1) to an inspector as they have effect in relation to the issue of a warrant under that provision to a constable.

(2) In their application in relation to the issue of a warrant under section 19(4) or 23(1), sections 15 and 16 of that Act shall have effect with the following modifications.

(3) In section 15—

(a) in subsection (2), omit the words from the end of paragraph (a)(ii) to the end of paragraph (b);

(b) omit subsections (2A) and (5A);

(c) in subsection (5), omit the words from "unless" to the end;

(d) in subsection (6)(a), omit the words from the end of sub-paragraph (iii) to the end of sub-paragraph (iv);

(e) in subsection (7), omit the words from "(see" to the end.

(4) In section 16—

(a) omit subsections (3A) and (3B);

(b) in subsection (9), omit the words after paragraph (b).

2 (1) This paragraph and paragraph 3 have effect in relation to the issue to inspectors of warrants under section 28(4); and an entry on premises under such a warrant is unlawful unless it complies with this paragraph and paragraph 3.

(2) Where an inspector applies for a warrant, he shall—

(a) state the ground on which he makes the application,

(b) state the enactment under which the warrant would be issued, and

(c) specify the premises which it is desired to enter.

(3) An application for a warrant shall be made without notice and supported by an information in writing.

(4) The inspector shall answer on oath any question that the justice of the peace hearing the application asks him.

(5) A warrant shall authorise an entry on one occasion only.

(6) A warrant shall specify—

(a) the name of the person who applies for it,

(b) the date on which it is issued, and

(c) the enactment under which it is issued.

(7) Two copies shall be made of a warrant.

(8) The copies shall be clearly certified as copies.

3 (1) A warrant may be executed by any inspector.

(2) A warrant may authorise persons to accompany any inspector who is executing it.

(3) A person authorised under sub-paragraph (2) has the same powers as the inspector whom he accompanies in respect of the execution of the warrant, but may exercise those powers only in the company, and under the supervision, of an inspector.

(4) Execution of a warrant must be within three months from the date of its issue.

(5) Execution of a warrant must be at a reasonable hour unless it appears to the inspector executing it that the purpose of entry may be frustrated on an entry at a reasonable hour.

(6) Where the occupier of premises which are to be entered under a warrant is present at the time when an inspector seeks to execute it, the inspector shall—

(a) identify himself to the occupier and shall produce to him documentary evidence that he is an inspector,

(b) produce the warrant to him, and

(c) supply him with a copy of it.

(7) Where—

(a) the occupier of premises which are to be entered under a warrant is not present when an inspector seeks to execute it, but

(b) some other person who appears to the inspector to be in charge of the premises is present,

sub-paragraph (6) shall have effect as if any reference to the occupier were a reference to that other person.

(8) If there is no person present who appears to the inspector to be in charge of the premises, he shall leave a copy of the warrant in a prominent place on the premises.

(9) A warrant which—

(a) has been executed, or

(b) has not been executed within the time authorised for its execution,

shall be returned to the designated officer for the local justice area in which the justice of the peace who issued the warrant was acting when he issued it.

(10) A warrant which is returned under sub-paragraph (9) shall be retained by the officer to whom it is returned for 12 months from its return.

(11) If during the period for which a warrant is to be retained the occupier of the premises to which it relates asks to inspect it, he shall be allowed to do so.

Duty to produce evidence of identity

4 (1) This paragraph applies to a power of entry conferred by section 19(1), 22(2), 26(2), 27(2), 28(2) or 29(2).

(2) A person may only exercise a power of entry to which this paragraph applies if on request—

(a) he produces evidence of his identity and of his entitlement to exercise the power;

(b) he outlines the purpose for which the power is exercised.

Power to take persons onto premises

5 In exercising a power to which paragraph 4 applies, a person may take with him onto the premises such persons as he thinks appropriate.

Duty to exercise power of entry at reasonable time

6 Entry under a power to which paragraph 4 applies shall be at a reasonable time, unless it appears to the person exercising the power that the purpose for which he is exercising the power would be frustrated on entry at a reasonable time.

Power to require assistance

7 (1) This paragraph applies to a power of entry conferred by—

(a) section 19(1), 22(2), 26(2), 27(2), 28(2) or 29(2), or

(b) a warrant under section 19(4), 22(4), 23(1) or 28(4).

(2) Where a person enters premises in the exercise of a power of entry to which this paragraph applies, he may require any qualifying person on the premises to give him such assistance as he may reasonably require for the purpose for which entry is made.

(3) The reference in sub-paragraph (2) to a qualifying person is to—

(a) the occupier of the premises;

(b) any person who appears to the person exercising the power to be responsible for animals on the premises;

(c) any person who appears to the person exercising the power to be under the direction or control of a person mentioned in paragraph (a) or (b).

(4) In the case of a power under section 26(2), the reference in sub-paragraph (2) to a qualifying person also includes the holder of a licence—

(a) specifying the premises as premises on which the carrying on of an activity is authorised, or

(b) relating to an activity which is being carried on on the premises.

Power to take equipment onto premises

8 In exercising a power to which paragraph 7 applies, a person may take with him such equipment and materials as he thinks appropriate.

Duty to leave premises secured

9 If, in the exercise of a power of entry to which paragraph 7 applies, a person enters premises which are unoccupied, he shall leave them as effectively secured against entry as he found them.

Functions in connection with inspection and search

10 (1) This paragraph applies to—

(a) a power of inspection conferred by section 26(1), 27(1), 28(1) or 29(1), and

(b) a power of search conferred by a warrant under section 23(1).

(2) A person exercising a power to which this paragraph applies may—

(a) inspect an animal found on the premises;

(b) inspect any other thing found on the premises, including a document or record (in whatever form it is held);

(c) carry out a measurement or test (including a measurement or test of an animal found on the premises);

(d) take a sample (including a sample from an animal found on the premises or from any substance on the premises which appears to be intended for use as food for such an animal);

(e) mark an animal found on the premises for identification purposes;

(f) remove a carcass found on the premises for the purpose of carrying out a post-mortem examination on it;

(g) take copies of a document or record found on the premises (in whatever form it is held);

(h) require information stored in an electronic form and accessible from the premises to be produced in a form in which it can be taken away and in which it is visible and legible or from which it can readily be produced in a visible and legible form;

(i) take a photograph of anything on the premises;

(j) seize and detain or remove anything which the person exercising the power reasonably believes to be evidence of any non-compliance, or of the commission of any offence, relevant to the purpose for which the inspection or search is made.

(3) A person taken onto premises under paragraph 5 may exercise any power conferred by sub-paragraph (2) if he is in the company, and under the supervision, of a person exercising a power to which this paragraph applies.

11 A person who takes a sample from an animal pursuant to paragraph 10(2)(d) shall give a part of the sample, or a similar sample, to any person appearing to be responsible for the animal, if, before the sample is taken, he is requested to do so by that person.

12 (1) Paragraph 10(2)(j) does not include power to seize an item which the person exercising the power has reasonable grounds for believing to be subject to legal privilege (within the meaning of section 10 of the Police and Criminal Evidence Act 1984 (c. 60)).

(2) A person who seizes anything in exercise of the power under paragraph 10(2)(j) shall on request provide a record of the thing seized to a person showing himself—

(a) to be the occupier of premises on which it was seized, or

(b) to have had possession or control of it immediately before its seizure.

(3) Subject to sub-paragraph (4), anything which has been seized in the exercise of a power under paragraph 10(2)(j) may be retained so long as is necessary in all the circumstances and in particular—

(a) for use as evidence at a trial for a relevant offence, or

(b) for forensic examination or for investigation in connection with a relevant offence.

(4) Nothing may be retained for either of the purposes mentioned in sub-paragraph (3) if a photograph or a copy would be sufficient for that purpose.

13 As soon as reasonably practicable after having exercised a power to which paragraph 10 applies, the person who exercised the power shall—

(a) prepare a written report of the inspection or search, and
(b) if requested to do so by the occupier of the premises, give him a copy of the report.

14 (1) A person exercising a power of search conferred by a warrant under section 23(1) may (if necessary) use reasonable force in the exercise of powers under paragraph 10 in connection with the execution of the warrant.

(2) A person carrying out an inspection under section 28(1) on premises which he is authorised to enter by a warrant under section 28(4) may (if necessary) use reasonable force in the exercise of powers under paragraph 10 in connection with the inspection.

Functions in connection with entry under section 19

15 (1) Where a person enters premises in exercise of a power of entry conferred by section 19(1), or by a warrant under section 19(4), he may—
(a) inspect an animal found on the premises;
(b) remove a carcass found on the premises for the purposes of carrying out a post-mortem examination on it;
(c) remove for those purposes the carcass of an animal destroyed on the premises in exercise of power conferred by section 18(3) or (4);
(d) take a photograph of anything on the premises.

(2) Where a person exercising a power of entry under section 19(1) takes another person with him under paragraph 5, the other person may exercise any power conferred by sub-paragraph (1) if he is in the company, and under the supervision, of the person exercising the power of entry.

Offences

16 A person commits an offence if he—
(a) intentionally obstructs a person in the lawful exercise of a power to which paragraph 7 or 10 applies;
(b) intentionally obstructs a person in the lawful exercise of a power conferred by this Schedule;
(c) fails without reasonable excuse to give any assistance which he is required to give under paragraph 7.

SCHEDULE 3

Section 64

MINOR AND CONSEQUENTIAL AMENDMENTS

Performing Animals (Regulation) Act 1925 (c. 38)

1 In section 4 of the Performing Animals (Regulation) Act 1925 (offences and legal proceedings), in subsection (2), after "enactment," insert "or of an offence under any of sections 4, 5, 6(1) and (2), 7 to 9 and 11 of the Animal Welfare Act 2006".

Cinematograph Films (Animals) Act 1937 (c. 59)

2 In section 1 of the Cinematograph Films (Animals) Act 1937 (prohibition of films involving cruelty to animals), in subsection (4), for paragraph (b) substitute—

"(b) in relation to England and Wales, the expression "animal" means a "protected animal" within the meaning of the Animal Welfare Act 2006."

Pet Animals Act 1951 (c. 35)

3 (1) Section 2 of the Pet Animals Act 1951 (pets not to be sold in streets etc.) ceases to have effect.

(2) In section 5 of that Act (offences and disqualifications), in subsection (3), after "1912," insert "or of any offence under any of sections 4, 5, 6(1) and (2), 7 to 9 and 11 of the Animal Welfare Act 2006,".

Protection of Animals (Amendment) Act 1954 (c. 40)

4 (1) In the Protection of Animals (Amendment) Act 1954, after section 2 insert—

"2A Breach of disqualification order

"2A Breach of disqualification order

(1) If a person has custody of any animal in contravention of an order made under this Act by a court in Scotland, he shall be liable on summary conviction to—

(a) imprisonment for a term not exceeding 51 weeks, or

(b) a fine not exceeding level 3 on the standard scale.

or to both.

(2) This section applies to orders made before, as well as to orders made after, the coming into force of this section."

(2) In relation to an offence under the inserted section 2A committed before the commencement of section 281(5) of the Criminal Justice Act 2003 (c. 44), the reference in subsection (1)(a) of the section to 51 weeks is to be read as a reference to 6 months.

Animal Boarding Establishments Act 1963 (c. 43)

5 (1) In section 1 of the Animal Boarding Establishments Act 1963 (licensing of boarding establishments for animals), in subsection (2), at the end of paragraph (e) insert "or—

(f) under section 34(2), (3) or (4) of the Animal Welfare Act 2006,".

(2) In section 3 of that Act (offences and disqualification), in subsection (3), after "1951," insert "or of any offence under any of sections 4, 5, 6(1) and (2), 7 to 9 and 11 of the Animal Welfare Act 2006,".

Riding Establishments Act 1964 (c. 70)

6 (1) In section 1 of the Riding Establishments Act 1964 (licensing of riding establishments), in subsection (2), at the end of paragraph (f) insert "or—

(g) under section 34(2), (3) or (4) of the Animal Welfare Act 2006".

(2) In section 4 of that Act (penalties and disqualification), in subsection (3), after "1963," insert "or of any offence under any of sections 4, 5, 6(1) and (2), 7 to 9 and 11 of the Animal Welfare Act 2006,".

Breeding of Dogs Act 1973 (c. 60)

7 In section 1 of the Breeding of Dogs Act 1973 (licensing of breeding establishments for dogs), in subsection (2), at the end of paragraph (f) insert "or—

(g) under section 34(2), (3) or (4) of the Animal Welfare Act 2006,".

Guard Dogs Act 1975 (c. 50)

8 In section 3 of the Guard Dogs Act 1975 (guard dog kennel licences), in subsection (4), after "1973," insert "or of an offence under any of sections 4, 5, 6(1) and (2), 7 to 9 and 11 of the Animal Welfare Act 2006,".

Dangerous Wild Animals Act 1976 (c. 38)

9 In section 6 of the Dangerous Wild Animals Act 1976 (penalties), in subsection (2)—

(a) for "Protection of Animals Acts 1911 to 1964," substitute "Protection of Animals Act 1911,",

(b) after "1912 to 1964," insert "the Performing Animals (Regulation) Act 1925,",

(c) after "1951," insert "the Animals (Cruel Poisons) Act 1962,", and

(d) after "1973," insert "or of an offence under any of sections 4, 5, 6(1) and (2), 7 to 9 and 11 of the Animal Welfare Act 2006,".

Magistrates' Courts Act 1980 (c. 43)

10 In section 108 of the Magistrates' Courts Act 1980 (right of appeal to the Crown Court), in subsection (3)(c), for "section 2 of the Protection of Animals Act 1911" substitute "section 37(1) of the Animal Welfare Act 2006".

Zoo Licensing Act 1981 (c. 37)

11 In section 4 of the Zoo Licensing Act 1981 (grant or refusal of licence), in subsection (5)—

(a) for "the Protection of Animals Acts 1911 to 1964" substitute "the Protection of Animals Act 1911",

(b) after the entry for the Protection of Animals (Scotland) Acts 1912 to 1964, insert—

"the Performing Animals (Regulation) Act 1925;",

(c) after the entry for the Pet Animals 1951, insert—

"the Animals (Cruel Poisons) Act 1962;", and

(d) at the end, insert—

"sections 4, 5, 6(1) and (2), 7 to 9 and 11 of the Animal Welfare Act 2006."

Animals (Scientific Procedures) Act 1986 (c. 14)

12 (1) In section 22(5) of the Animals (Scientific Procedures) Act 1986 (penalties for contraventions)—

(a) for "section 1 of the Protection of Animals Act 1911" substitute "any of sections 4, 5, 6(1) and (2), 7 and 8 of the Animal Welfare Act 2006", and

(b) at the end insert "(rather than any penalty by way of imprisonment or fine provided for in those Acts)".

(2) In section 26 of that Act (prosecutions), in subsection (1)(b), for "section 1 of the Protection of Animals Act 1911" substitute "any of sections 4, 5, 6(1) and (2) and 7 to 9 of the Animal Welfare Act 2006".

(3) In section 29 of that Act (application to Northern Ireland), for subsection (5) substitute—

"(5) In section 22(5) above for the reference to sections 4, 5, 6(1) and (2), 7 and 8 of the Animal Welfare Act 2006 there shall be substituted a reference to sections 13 and 14 of the Welfare of Animals Act (Northern Ireland) 1972.

(5A) In section 26(1)(b) above for the reference to sections 4, 5, 6(1) and (2) and 7 to 9 of the Animal Welfare Act 2006 there shall be substituted a reference to sections 13 and 14 of the Welfare of Animals Act (Northern Ireland) 1972."

Wild Mammals (Protection) Act 1996 (c. 3)

13 For section 3 of the Wild Mammals (Protection) Act 1996 (interpretation) substitute—

"3 Interpretation

"3 Interpretation

In this Act "wild mammal" means any mammal which is not a "protected animal" within the meaning of the Animal Welfare Act 2006."

Criminal Justice and Police Act 2001 (c. 16)

14 (1) In section 57 of the Criminal Justice and Police Act 2001 (retention of seized items), in subsection (1), at the end insert—

"(r) paragraph 12(3) of Schedule 2 to the Animal Welfare Act 2006."

(2) In section 66 of that Act (general interpretation of Part 2), in subsection (4), at the end insert—

"(p) sections 26(1), 27(1), 28(1) and 29(1) of the Animal Welfare Act 2006 (inspection in connection with licences, inspection in connection with registration, inspection of farm premises and inspection relating to Community obligations)."

(3) In Part 1 of Schedule 1 to that Act (powers of seizure to which section 50 applies), at the end insert—

"Animal Welfare Act 2006

73I The power of seizure conferred by paragraph 10(2)(j) of Schedule 2 to the Animal Welfare Act 2006."

SCHEDULE 4

Section 65

REPEALS

Short title and chapter	*Extent of repeal*
Metropolitan Police Act 1839 (c. 47)	Section 47.
Town Police Clauses Act 1847 (c. 89)	Section 36.
Protection of Animals Act 1911 (c. 27)	Sections 1 to 3, 5 to 5B, 7, 9 and 11 to 14.
	In section 15, paragraphs (a), (c), (e) and (f).
Protection of Animals (1911) Amendment Act 1921 (c. 14)	The whole Act.
Protection of Animals Act 1934 (c. 21)	The whole Act.
Docking and Nicking of Horses Act 1949 (c. 70)	Section 1.
	In section 3, the definition of "nicking".
Pet Animals Act 1951 (c. 35)	Sections 2 and 3.
Cockfighting Act 1952 (c. 59)	The whole Act.
Protection of Animals (Amendment) Act 1954 (c. 40)	Sections 1, 2 and 4(1).
Protection of Animals (Anaesthetics) Act 1954 (c. 46)	The whole Act.
Abandonment of Animals Act 1960 (c. 43)	The whole Act.
Animals (Cruel Poisons) Act 1962 (c. 26)	In section 4(2), the words from "and the Protection of Animals Acts 1911" to "and this Act".
Protection of Animals (Anaesthetics) Act 1964 (c. 39)	The whole Act.
Agriculture (Miscellaneous Provisions) Act 1968 (c. 34)	Part 1.
Animal Health Act 1981 (c. 22)	Sections 37 to 39.
	In Schedule 5, paragraph 8.
Animals (Scientific Procedures) Act 1986 (c. 14)	In Schedule 3, paragraphs 1 and 7.
Protection of Animals (Penalties) Act 1987 (c. 35)	The whole Act.

Status: *This is the original version (as it was originally enacted).*

Short title and chapter	*Extent of repeal*
Protection of Animals (Amendment) Act 1988 (c. 29)	Section 1. In section 2— (a) in subsection (1), the words "section 47 of the Metropolitan Police Act 1839," and the words "and section 36 of the Town Police Clauses Act 1847", and (b) subsection (2).
Protection against Cruel Tethering Act 1988 (c. 31)	The whole Act.
Protection of Animals (Amendment) Act 2000 (c. 40)	The whole Act.

GRANGIS - UK PUBLISHING 2022.

Thank you for taking the time to leave us a review regarding this version

★★★★★

For further inquiries, contact us at:
www.grangis.com / contact@grangis.com

www.ingramcontent.com/pod-product-compliance
Lightning Source LLC
LaVergne TN
LVHW060214210926
848481LV00008B/2738